ZAHA HADID
BUILDING THE FUTURE

Jo Nelson

OXFORD
UNIVERSITY PRESS

CONTENTS

INTRODUCING ZAHA HADID

Dame Zaha Hadid was one of the world's most famous **architects**. She became known for her daring designs, using sharp angles and swooping curves.

Zaha Hadid stands outside one of the buildings she designed: the Riverside Museum of Transport in Glasgow, Scotland. The zigzag roof is designed to look like a wave, flowing from the city on one side to the waterfront on the other side.

LONDON AQUATICS CENTRE

A PLAN FOR A NEW PROJECT IN SERBIA

ROSENTHAL CENTER
FOR CONTEMPORARY
ARTS, CINCINNATI

MAXXI MUSEUM, ROME

GUANGZHOU OPERA HOUSE, CHINA

Zaha's architectural designs became extremely popular all over the world. However, for many years, nobody would build her buildings. People thought they were too complicated and too expensive. So just how did Zaha become a world-famous architect?

CHILDHOOD DREAMS

Zaha was born in Iraq in 1950. Zaha's father was an important **politician** and Zaha was surrounded by interesting, successful people.

One of her father's friends was an architect. When Zaha was six he designed a house for her aunt. He brought sketches and a model to show the family. Zaha took one look at the model and was immediately inspired.

As a child, Zaha loved drawing and sketching. By the age of 11, she had decided that she wanted to be an architect too.

Iraq in 1950

When Zaha was a child, she visited Córdoba in Spain with her parents. She stood in the **Great Mosque** and gazed at the **vast** structure around her. It was a very old building, but it looked so modern. Zaha was impressed. It was one of the buildings that inspired her most.

Over 50 years later, Zaha designed this International Culture and Arts Centre in Changsha, China.

STARTING OUT

Zaha knew she wanted to be an architect, but how would she achieve this dream?

To become an architect, you have to study for four or five years. Then you have to work for two years in an architect's office.

1968-1971

Studied Mathematics at the American University in Beirut, Lebanon.

1972-1977

Studied at the Architectural Association in London. One of her most inspiring teachers was Rem Koolhaas.

Rem Koolhaas is a Dutch writer and architect. He taught a daring new approach to design. He matched design to the way people live in the modern world.

A sketch of the Dutch parliament buildings. Rem Koolhaas designed the extension.

1977 - 1979
Worked for Rem Koolhaas at the Office for Metropolitan Architecture.

1977
Won the prize for best student and graduated. Became a teacher at the Architectural Association.

1980
Founded Zaha Hadid Architects.

WINNING COMPETITIONS

Architects often get their first big break by winning a competition to design a new building.

In 1983, Zaha did just that. She beat 538 other entries in a competition to design a leisure centre in Hong Kong. Usually architects do line drawings and make models of their designs. Zaha did paintings as well to get her ideas across to the judges.

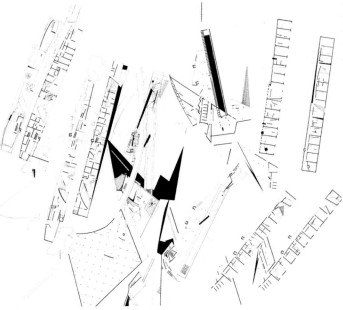

This is a painting by Zaha for her leisure centre.

Unfortunately, the **developers** in Hong Kong ran out of money and the leisure centre was never built.

In 1994, Zaha won a competition to design an opera house in Cardiff. Her design was bold and exciting. It was nicknamed 'the crystal necklace'.

Zaha presented her opera house design through paintings, sketches and models.

This is a 3D model of the Cardiff Bay Opera House.

Sadly, this building was never built either. The people in charge worried that it was too **ambitious** and expensive. They decided that the money should be spent on building something else instead.

LIFT OFF

Zaha had been an architect for over ten years, but none of her buildings had been built. She had found her own **distinctive** style. Her designs were catching people's attention. Now she needed a **client** to believe in her and finish a project.

Finally her first design was built. It was a fire station in Germany.

VITRA FIRE STATION, GERMANY

Next came a **tram** station in France and a ski jump in Austria. Zaha's ski jump includes a 50 metre tower with a cafe at the top.

Zaha wanted the ski jump to extend the mountainside into the sky above.

Then, in 1997, Zaha was asked to design a modern art museum in Cincinnati, United States of America. The building was completed in 2003. Finally, Zaha's career had really taken off!

ROSENTHAL CENTER FOR CONTEMPORARY ARTS, CINCINNATI

Zaha's museum in Cincinnati won her an architectural award, the Pritzker Prize. She was the first woman to win this prize.

FULL SPEED AHEAD

After Zaha's success in Cincinnati, more jobs came flooding in. These included an impressive building at a BMW car factory.

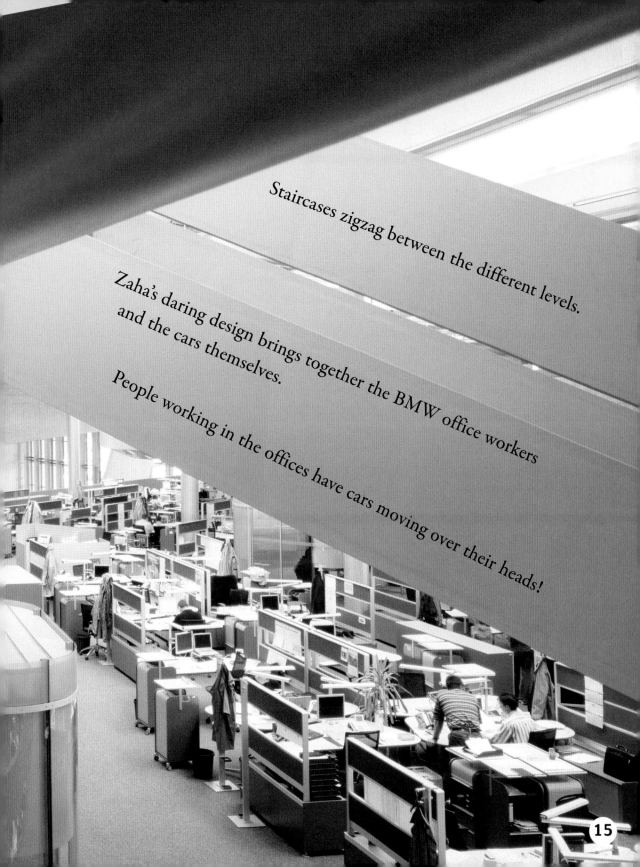

Staircases zigzag between the different levels.

Zaha's daring design brings together the BMW office workers and the cars themselves.

People working in the offices have cars moving over their heads!

15

ZAHA'S OFFICE

Zaha's company **employed** several hundred people. They worked on hundreds of projects in over 40 countries.

Zaha's office was in an old school building in London. If you walked past, you would never know that dazzling buildings were being designed inside.

Architects used to draw designs with a pencil and ruler on paper. Today, architects use computers and create 3D models. Zaha's designs were so complicated, they could not have been developed without computer technology.

Zaha's buildings were designed by a large team of **professionals**, all working together.

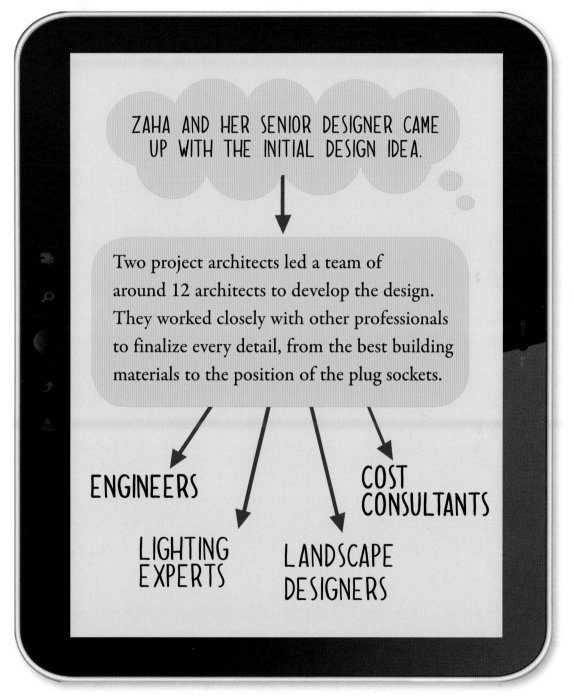

ZAHA AND HER SENIOR DESIGNER CAME UP WITH THE INITIAL DESIGN IDEA.

Two project architects led a team of around 12 architects to develop the design. They worked closely with other professionals to finalize every detail, from the best building materials to the position of the plug sockets.

ENGINEERS

COST CONSULTANTS

LIGHTING EXPERTS

LANDSCAPE DESIGNERS

Finally, the design was ready to be built.

BUILDING THE BUILDINGS

It took hundreds of people to construct one of Zaha's buildings. Her design for the London Aquatics Centre at the 2012 Olympics took three years to build.

THE MASSIVE CURVED ROOF WAS CONSTRUCTED ON THE GROUND FIRST

Architects do not just design the outside of buildings. They choose all of the inside details too, from the seats to the door handles.

This is the dive pool for the completed aquatics centre.

BEFORE BEING HOISTED INTO PLACE.

AQUATICS CENTRE FACTS

- IT IS 160 METRES LONG. THAT IS LONGER THAN FIVE BLUE WHALES.
- THE ROOF WEIGHS 2800 TONNES. THAT IS HEAVIER THAN 18 BLUE WHALES.
- THERE ARE THREE POOLS. TOGETHER THEY HOLD AROUND 10 MILLION LITRES OF WATER.

DESIGN DETAILS

Zaha continued to create amazing buildings, but she used her design skills to create other objects too.

She designed furniture ...

This is called the liquid glacial table because it resembles water and ice.

several jewellery collections ...

shoes that share the same curves as her buildings ...

luxury yachts …

and an unusual doll's house.

"When people see something fantastic they think that it's not possible to achieve it in real life. But that's not true. You can achieve amazing things."

GLOSSARY

ambitious: wanting to achieve something and to be successful

architects: people who design buildings

client: someone who pays another person for advice or a service

cost consultants: people who work out how much a building costs to build

developers: people who construct or convert buildings

distinctive: unusual, easily recognizable

employed: gave someone a job

engineers: people who plan or make things like machines or bridges

founded: set up a company or an organization

glacial: icy

Great Mosque: place of worship in Spain

politician: someone who works in politics

professionals: trained people who are experts at their jobs

tram: an electric train that runs on rails set into the street

vast: very big

INDEX

Dame Zaha Hadid
Born: 31 October 1950 in Baghdad, Iraq
Died: 31 March 2016 in Miami, United States of America

ABOUT THE AUTHOR

I'm a children's author and I'm married to an architect. We've lived together in some extremely interesting places, from a converted church to an old farmhouse, and now we live in a very modern house. So a book about Zaha Hadid was perfect for me!

As well as writing books, I run writing workshops and I often visit primary schools and talk to children about writing. I reckon adults can learn a lot from children about being inquisitive and creative.

Greg Foot, Series Editor

I've loved science ever since the day I took my papier mâché volcano into school. I filled it with far too much baking powder, vinegar and red food colouring, and WHOOSH! I covered the classroom ceiling in red goo. Now I've got the best job in the world: I present TV shows for the BBC, answer kids' science questions on YouTube, and make huge explosions on stage at festivals!

Working on TreeTops inFact has been great fun. There are so many brilliant books, and guess what ... they're all packed full of awesome facts! What's your favourite?